The Library Instruction Round Table of the American Library Association provides a forum for discussing library instruction issues pertinent to all types of libraries, including academic, public, school, and corporate. Persons interested in membership in LIRT should send inquiries to the American Library Association, Membership Services, 50 E. Huron St., Chicago, IL 60611, or call (800) 545-2433.

EVALUATING LIBRARY INSTRUCTION LIBRARIANS

AND PROGRAMS: CASE STUDIES

by the

Continuing Education Committee

Library Instruction Round Table

American Library Association

Edited by

Christopher W. Nolan

1991

CONTENTS

INTRODUCTION

Trish Ridgeway

The Issue of Evaluation

Librarians who assist patrons in learning to effectively use libraries and information engage in a wide variety of activities: determining client needs, designing programs and materials to meet these needs, and then marketing programs and services to their clientele. Too often bibliographic instruction librarians expend all their effort in these activities. They may have no time to evaluate their activities; or they perform perfunctory evaluations; or they evaluate their programs but make little use of the evaluation results.

Yet, evaluation in this era of accountability can provide librarians with the tools and information to improve: evaluation will help determine if clients' needs have been met and if there are other needs that have not yet been addressed; evaluation will provide the information necessary to improve programs and materials; and evaluation results will give librarians data to show patrons and administrators how their instructional activities are helping to meet library users' information needs.

So why don't bibliographic instruction librarians make more use of evaluation techniques? They don't because evaluation is difficult,[1] because the evaluation of personnel may cause hard feelings, and because evaluation results may yield information they don't want to know. The cases in this book deal with the dilemmas related to the evaluation of instructional services in a variety of settings. The questions that follow each case provide examples of the issues librarians must face in order to establish effective evaluation practices.

How to Use This Casebook

The authors of these cases envisioned them being used in a number of ways: in library school instruction, in conference programs and continuing education workshops, in in-service programs within a library or school district, or by an individual who seeks to learn more on the topic of evaluation.

In classroom or workshop settings the number of ways these case studies may be used is limited only by the imagination of the participants. For example, workshop planners could select one case to present or to act out and then have general discussion or small group discussion on the case. In a half-day or day-long workshop participants could use the entire casebook and divide into small groups with each group discussing and then presenting a different case to the entire group. A single case could be the focus of a conference program. A case scenario could be presented live or via videotape to attendees, followed by a panel discussion or small group discussion. Program coordinators who plan to use a case study are encouraged to call the author of that case study if they wish to discuss it in greater detail.

In whatever manner individuals choose to use these cases, they should keep in mind the main intent of the authors of the casebook--to stimulate discussion of the effective evaluation of library instruction and to encourage instruction librarians to incorporate evaluation into their programs.

1. Mignon Adams in a 1987 LOEX presentation presents some excellent suggestions for making evaluation less painful: see her "Evaluation for Teaching Effectiveness," in *Defining and Applying Effective Teaching Strategies for Library Instruction: Papers Presented at the 14th [i.e., 15th] Library Instruction Conference Held at Ohio State University, 7 & 8 May, 1987*, edited by Mary Beth Bunge and Teresa B. Mensching, p. 13-16 (Ann Arbor: Pierian Press, 1989).

EVALUATION OF INSTRUCTION LIBRARIANS

THE ROLE OF THE BIBLIOGRAPHIC INSTRUCTION COORDINATOR
IN PERSONNEL EVALUATION

Trish Ridgeway

Helen Jones came to Midwest University over two years ago to take on the newly-created position of Bibliographic Instruction Coordinator. Her first task was to formulate a campus-wide plan for library instruction, which she did with a committee of librarians representing many of the libraries on campus. Her job responsibilities include putting the plan for library instruction into action; teaching bibliographic instruction sessions; helping librarians prepare instructional materials; and designing campus-wide orientation and instructional materials in printed, audio-visual and computer program formats.

Although she doesn't have any formal supervisory responsibilities, Helen's job description also states that she will observe the teaching of each librarian in the program at least twice a year and help each one work out a plan to improve his or her teaching. When all positions are filled, there are nineteen librarians who teach in the Midwest BI program.

Helen was on her way to a meeting with her boss, Mary Welles, when she spotted Jill Johnson. Jill has been a reference librarian in the main library, her first professional position, for about a year and a half.

"Jill, wait a minute. I want to hear how your session with that political science class went."

Jill stopped and frowned. "Oh, Helen, I don't know. I really prepared for the class, but when it was over I wasn't sure that anybody learned anything. Remember I told you that this is Professor Barnes' course for undergraduates, Introduction to Political Science Research and Methods? I've been trying to get him to bring this class to the library for an instructional session for some time; reaching this class is a major objective of our BI outreach plan. But I think I blew it. I have another section of the course in two days, and if it doesn't go any better, I don't think he'll ever ask for another library lecture."

"Jill, I can't believe it went that badly. I've seen some of your freshman composition presentations, and they were great!"

Jill sighed, "But, you know, in them I just follow the outline. I've never had to design a session entirely from scratch. Maybe I tried to cover too much, but there are so many important sources they should know about."

"Are you free at three today?" Helen asked. Jill nodded yes. "Why don't we meet and look at your objectives and outline for the class?"

"Helen, I'm afraid I didn't have time to write down any objectives. Of course, I mainly wanted them to learn about the basic political science resources."

"Okay, Jill, we'll start with that. See you at three in my office, okay?" Jill agreed, and Helen continued on down the hall to Mary Welles' office. Mary Welles is the Head of Public Services and Helen's direct supervisor.

"Hi, Mary, sorry I'm late, but I was just giving moral support to Jill Johnson. She's designing a teaching session on her own for the first time."

"So, how is she doing?"

"She's shaky, but I think with a little more work she'll do fine."

Mary leaned back in her chair. "You've done such a good job coordinating our bibliographic instruction program that I'd like to give you a little more responsibility."

Helen felt both apprehensive and eager. "Thanks for the compliment. What do you have in mind?"

"Well, in the two years you've been here you've demonstrated your special expertise in instructional design and in improving teaching; you're the natural one to evaluate the teaching of everyone who participates in BI."

"I really do that already. I mean I observe everyone a couple times a year and meet with each person to discuss setting up a plan to improve some aspect of their teaching.

Several people have asked me to work with them on specific problem areas, and slowly people are agreeing to be videotaped..."

"Helen, sorry to interrupt, but what I mean is to *formally* evaluate staff members."

"Mary, I'm not sure I . . ."

"We evaluate people on job performance, and for some staff bibliographic instruction is a sizable part of their jobs. The department heads want your input when they do annual performance evaluations. You do agree you know more about the teaching effectiveness of our BI instructors than anyone else?"

Helen slumped a little lower in her chair. "Well, yes . . . I suppose I could meet with the department heads and give them some feedback."

"No, Helen, what we really would like you to do is design a form that uses the same evaluative statements as our general form. You know, 'far exceeds expectations,' 'exceeds expectations,' etc."

"Oh, Mary, this makes me very uncomfortable. I'm not sure people would come to me with their teaching problems if they knew I'd be evaluating them. My collegial approach has worked well with just about everyone. Am I supposed to share this form with them? I just don't know."

Mary frowned and shifted some papers on her desk. "Helen, I'm really surprised at this reaction. What about Steven? You were just complaining last week that he wouldn't accept any advice from you even though his teaching was awful. How did you describe him--disorganized and what else?"

"Disorganized yet pedantic," Helen supplied glumly.

"Right! And you thought he'd never change because you weren't his supervisor. And you've said that about a few other people too, haven't you? Wasn't Celia one? And who else was there?" Mary asked.

"Jim Tate," Helen said. "I know I complained about a few people who don't really want to participate in our overall BI plan or who don't want any suggestions on how to improve. I did say if I had some direct control over them, that perhaps it would make a difference. But now I'm worried about *everyone else*. Will they feel free to confide in me if they know I'll be preparing a written evaluation?"

"Everyone in supervisory positions has these problems," Helen replied. "You're just going to have to bite the bullet and do it. I'd like to have a preliminary evaluation form from you before the Public Services department heads' meeting on the 17th of next month. Let me take a look at it by the 15th, and then you can attend the meeting and present it to the department heads."

QUESTIONS FOR DISCUSSION

1. Was Mary Welles right in requesting Helen to prepare a formal evaluation instrument?

2. Do you think formal written evaluation by Helen of the librarians' bibliographic instruction skills will impede her ability to work as a peer consultant and coach to the librarians in the program? What do you think the impact of evaluation will be on Jill Johnson and Steven?

3. Since Helen does not seem to have any choice but to provide evaluation information, how should she go about designing an evaluation instrument?

4. How should she structure the evaluation process so that the end result is the improvement of teaching?

ADDITIONAL READING

Broidy, Ellen. "Organizational Structure: Politics, Problems, and Challenges." In "Library Literacy" column, edited by Mary Reichel. *RQ* 28 (Winter 1988): 162-68.

Clark, Alice S., and Kay F. Jones, eds. *Teaching Librarians to Teach: On-the-Job Training for Bibliographic Instruction Librarians.* Metuchen, New Jersey: Scarecrow, 1986.

Menges, Robert J. *Colleagues as Catalysts for Change in Teaching.* Paper presented at the Annual Meeting of the American Educational Research Association (70th, San Francisco, April 16-20, 1986). Reston, Virginia.: EDRS, 1986. (ED 270 406)

Performance Evaluation in Reference Services in ARL Libraries. Spec Kit, no. 139. Washington, D.C.: Association of Research Libraries, Office of Management Studies, November-December 1987.

Ridgeway, Trish. "Changing Teaching Styles." In "Library Literacy" column, edited by Mary Reichel. *RQ* 29 (Fall 1989): 24-27.

Wildman, Terry M., and Jerry A. Niles. "Essentials of Professional Growth." *Educational Leadership* 44 (February 1987): 4-10.

SEEING IS BELIEVING: EVALUATION BY VIDEOTAPE

Rebecca Jackson

Gabe Franks was the Coordinator for Bibliographic Instruction for a large public university. The library system had a total of seven libraries, with about thirty librarians involved in bibliographic instruction. Gabe was responsible for the instruction programs for all of these libraries, and he also contributed to the performance evaluations for each of these thirty librarians.

In the two years that Gabe had been in his position, he had attended several workshops on videotaping librarians' instruction sessions as a means of evaluation. Gabe decided to try this method for himself. After all, he had videotaping equipment available through the audiovisual department of the library, so taping would be no problem.

First Gabe checked with his supervisor to make sure she would have no problems with his plan. Once she approved it, he sent memos to all librarians involved in instruction, explaining the project and asking them to sign up for particular times. His plan was to start with simulated sessions. Each librarian would take ten minutes to present one aspect of his or her instruction in one of the instruction rooms. No students would be present. He felt that such simulation would alleviate problems with scheduling the videotaping sessions and might also keep some librarians from panicking at their first videotaping session.

After he sent out the memo, he developed a checklist of behaviors to look for in the sessions. This list was a compilation of several sample lists he had received in the workshops he had attended. The completed list was about two pages long.

Next he contacted the audiovisual department to learn how to do the taping. He had decided to do it himself, so that he and the librarian doing the session would be the

9

only ones present at the time of the taping. He discovered that taping was probably the simplest part of the whole project.

When he started receiving the forms from the librarians with their preferred times, he began to keep a schedule. He sent a copy to the audiovisual department for its scheduling of equipment and also sent a copy to the librarians.

He was confident everything was moving smoothly as the first day of scheduled taping arrived. He taped three librarians that day and followed a fairly simple procedure with each one. When they arrived for their sessions, he spoke with them for a few minutes about what they were planning to do. Then he started running the tape. At the end of ten minutes, he signaled the librarian that his or her time was up. Then Gabe and the librarian immediately watched the tape, both with the checklist in front of them. Finally, they discussed the session with reference to the checklist.

After the first day's sessions, Gabe was encouraged. However, he started hearing rumblings from the staff. Several of them had not yet signed up and did not want to. Since Gabe was not the supervisor for any of them, he had no authority to make them sign up. Then he began hearing that the librarians felt his checklist was too detailed and unfair. Several of them said that they would rather be doing an actual class--that faking a classroom situation would make them more uncomfortable than teaching a real class. Finally, they all wanted to know how the tapes were going to be used and what kind of follow-up Gabe was planning.

Gabe was disappointed. He was convinced that videotaping was a great way for librarians to see themselves and for him to spend some time with each of them discussing their special instructional problems and strengths. However, he felt he was getting no cooperation from the librarians. He just didn't know how to proceed.

QUESTIONS FOR DISCUSSION

1. How could Gabe have dealt with the refusal of librarians to sign up for the videotaping?

2. What items should be included in a checklist to be used in videotaping library instruction sessions to make it simple yet effective?

3. How could Gabe have enlisted support for the project?

4. What kinds of follow-up activities would be good to maintain interest in this method of evaluation?

5. How can Gabe use this evaluation method in his performance evaluations of librarians?

6. How can Gabe salvage this project?

ADDITIONAL READING

Ajayi, Dopemu Y., and J. K. Talabi. "The Effects of Videotape Recording on Microteaching Training Techniques for Education Students." *Journal of Educational Television* 12 (no. 1, 1986): 39-44.

Ellington, Jane C., and Harry C. Mayhew. "Sight, Sound, Action: Microteaching Experiences for Vocational Home Economics Students." *Clearing-House* 59 (February 1986): 275-76.

Frager, Alan M. "Video Technology and Teacher Training: A Research Perspective." *Educational Technology* 25 (July 1985): 20-22.

Franck, Marion R., and Michael A. DeSousa. "Foreign TAs: A Course in Communication Skills." *Improving College and University Teaching* 30 (Summer 1982): 111-14.

Ramey, M., and A. Spanjer. "Videotaping Bibliographic Instruction: A Confrontation with Self." *Research Strategies* 2 (Spring 1984): 71-75.

WHAT ARE YOU REALLY EVALUATING: ATTITUDE OR LEARNING?

Scott Davis

When Marny became Coordinator of Library Instruction at Druid University several months ago, she quickly realized that she had inherited a strong library instruction program. Her predecessor had been extremely well-organized and had developed a good collection of instructional handouts. About the only problem Marny could find with the program had to do with evaluation. Apparently, formal program evaluation had not been a priority in the past. One of the first things Marny did was set up a systematic method for gathering input from students and faculty members who participated in library instruction activities.

Marny's primary clientele at Druid University consists of sections of first-year English composition students. Marny schedules library instruction sessions at faculty members' requests. Sessions are usually of the 50-minute, "one-shot" variety; however, some faculty members allow two sessions. The usual content for these sessions consists of a brief introduction to the library's online catalog and an overview of periodical indexes. Marny uses hands-on exercises for the catalog and a separate exercise for indexes. Students complete these assignments outside of class and return them to Marny's office for scoring; Marny then corrects and returns them to the class instructor. About three-fourths of the English teachers who schedule library instruction sessions require their students to complete one or more of these hands-on exercises.

Since Marny's time with the students is so limited, she developed an evaluation instrument that students could respond to quickly. She usually allows 5 to 10 minutes at the end of each session to administer the evaluation. The evaluation includes such items as: Was the instruction session a worthwhile use of class time? Were the handouts helpful in terms of clarifying information presented in the session? Was the instruction librarian well-organized in her presentation? The evaluation also includes items allowing students to identify the most positive and negative aspects of the session and to make any general comments.

For faculty members, Marny developed an evaluation that she gives to them at the beginning of the session, asking them to complete it at their earliest convenience and return it to her in the self-addressed campus mail envelope attached to it. The faculty evaluation includes basically the same items as the student evaluation, but also addresses such areas as: Were there any problems in scheduling the session for the date and time the instructors needed? Were their ideas and suggestions used by the instruction librarian in the presentation? Would they recommend library instruction to their colleagues?

At the end of her first semester, Marny was extremely pleased with the overwhelmingly positive reaction of students and faculty to their library instruction experience. Students frequently added comments to their evaluations suggesting that all first-year students should be required to participate in a library instruction session.

When Marny visited with Ms. Lambert, the Head of Reference, for her six-month performance review, she had many good things to say about Marny's performance thus far. In discussing Marny's newly implemented evaluation procedure, Ms. Lambert was particularly pleased with Marny's initiative. However, during the course of their conversation Ms. Lambert raised an interesting point that had not occurred to Marny: since Marny's evaluation was administered immediately following the instruction session, students had not yet had an opportunity to apply the things that Marny had covered in class. While the students' *attitudes* might be positive immediately following the session, had they in fact *learned* anything? Might their positive attitude change over the course of the semester as they began to research their papers? Should Marny consider a follow-up, *ex post facto* evaluation by students and faculty, conducted near the end of the semester?

Ms. Lambert asked Marny to think of ways to expand and improve her current evaluation system. Marny left their meeting feeling good about the challenge ahead of her.

QUESTIONS FOR DISCUSSION

1. Are student perceptions and attitudes immediately following an instruction session valid measures of a BI program's health?

2. In many cases, students do not immediately appreciate the importance of a library instruction exercise or activity. Might this make their initial perceptions/attitudes about BI irrelevant to the BI librarian? Why or why not?

3. Is a combination of immediate attitudinal evaluation and *ex post facto* evaluation better than just one or the other? Would you say that either one is better than no form of evaluation at all?

4. Is student input regarding library instruction programs and activities more or less important than faculty input?

5. To what extent should Marny rely on student exercise scores as a measure of what students had learned?

6. How might Marny determine the impact of BI on students' composition course assignments?

ADDITIONAL READING

Freedman, Janet, and Harold Bantly. "Does It Work? Program Evaluation." In *Information Searching: A Handbook for Designing and Creating Instructional Programs*, p. 178-84. Metuchen, New Jersey: Scarecrow Press, 1982.

Freedman, Janet, and Harold Bantly. "Techniques of Program Evaluation." In *Teaching Librarians to Teach: On-the-Job Training for Bibliographic Instruction Librarians*, edited by Alice S. Clark and Kay F. Jones, p. 188-204. Metuchen, New Jersey: Scarecrow Press, 1986.

Johnson, Richard R. "Library Instruction: The Mythology of Evaluation." In *Evaluating Library Use Instruction: Papers Presented at the University of Denver Conference on the Evaluation of Library Instruction, December 13-14, 1973,* edited by Richard J. Beeler, p. 31-41. Ann Arbor, Michigan: Pierian Press, 1975.

Lubans, John, Jr. "Evaluation Attempts of Library Use Instruction Programs at the University of Colorado Libraries." In *Evaluating Library Use Instruction: Papers Presented at the University of Denver Conference on the Evaluation of Library Instruction, December 13-14, 1973,* edited by Richard J. Beeler, p. 67-73. Ann Arbor, Michigan: Pierian Press, 1975.

Roberts, Anne F. "Measuring the Results." In *Library Instruction for Librarians*, p. 84-89. Littleton, Colorado: Libraries Unlimited, 1982.

FACULTY EVALUATION OF BIBLIOGRAPHIC INSTRUCTION

Christopher W. Nolan

"Librarians don't really understand what our students need to read. Their job is to teach students how to find the materials that we think are important." Robert was caught off guard by these blunt remarks from Professor Nelson. He had been discussing an instructional session for her "Introduction to Psychological Research Methods" course that he had taught the previous semester. Student evaluations for the session had been quite favorable. But Robert had also initiated a procedure to ask for written evaluations of BI from the classroom instructors, and Judy Nelson had included quite a few critical comments. None of his other evaluations from faculty had included any major negative comments.

Robert had discussed his evaluations with his supervisor. She was particularly concerned about Nelson's negative comments and indicated to Robert that he was expected to change his approach in order to gain Judy's approval. "Word of mouth is so important for our BI program," she had said, "that we need to address any criticism immediately." Concerned about Judy's perceptions and his boss's attitude, he had promptly scheduled a meeting with Professor Nelson to let her elaborate on her views.

"I don't think that teaching students to use tools like *Psychological Abstracts* and *Social Sciences Index* is particularly useful," she continued. "In the first place, undergraduates can't distinguish good articles from the marginal--so their time is spent rummaging through a lot of irrelevant information. Second, scholars don't do their own research like librarians. I rarely use indexes; I follow up on the papers I see cited in current journals, or talk to my colleagues and find out what they're doing. So why teach them these sources, when it so often leads them in the wrong direction?"

"If they don't use the bibliographic tools, how do you expect them to find information for their papers?" Robert asked.

"Well, I expect them to ask me about important authors they can start with. Then they can look through the review journals and get some evaluative information about the literature."

Robert was puzzled. "But this is a research methods course. Surely we want our students to learn to find information on their own. When I talk about search strategies to the class, I try to emphasize using psychology encyclopedias, book reviews, and the citation indexes as ways to evaluate and find the important literature. What do you think is appropriate for me to cover, if I don't discuss these sources?"

"The main thing," Judy responded, "is how to find the periodicals in the library. But I would like them to try using the *Social Sciences Citation Index*--that gives them some experience seeing how researchers cite each other's works. But I wouldn't go into all that other stuff you covered last time. When you come in to talk to them this semester, I'd appreciate your leaving out everything except these few ideas."

As Robert reviewed the conversation with this professor later in his office, he had mixed feelings about her assessment of his instructional efforts. He appreciated hearing what she thought her students needed, and he usually tried to match his content with goals determined between the classroom teacher and himself. He was prepared for some potential criticism of elements such as his speaking style, use of appropriate level materials, or particular choices in reference tools. In fact, his request for written evaluations from the teaching faculty was meant to solicit such suggestions for improvement.

On the other hand, he was alarmed by her casual dismissal of the points he thought important to make in a class presentation. Contrary to Judy's critique, Robert thought psychology majors should be aware of, and use, the principal indexing tools in the field. Students might be overwhelmed when first using *Psychological Abstracts*, but he felt it important that students be exposed to it.

Moreover, Robert felt that his credibility as an instructor was in question. He had attempted to seek out the professor's perspective of her students' needs and make his talk appropriate to the students' assignment, yet he had certain points that he thought were necessary to make regardless of the professor's opinion. He felt that he was asked to speak to the class because of his expertise, like other guest lecturers. It was unlikely that Professor Nelson would ask another classroom teacher to change his lecture in the same way.

Robert decided, as he began to outline a revised class presentation, that a compromise between his and Judy's approaches might be the best alternative. Her research style, he concluded, was actually common among faculty and was therefore useful to convey to the students. He would describe the method, give examples from the citation index, and show the students how to find the references found with that method. But the subject search strategy he normally explained to the class was still important, so he would present it as an alternative, but not superior or inferior, method of doing a literature review. He thought it best to include more information on evaluating the information found through the reference sources, so that the students could concentrate on better quality sources.

This should appease Judy's concerns, he thought. He toyed with the idea of presenting this lecture without any additional discussion with her, but decided that might be risky. So he scheduled another appointment to discuss this approach. He resolved to insist that his concerns be included, although diplomacy would obviously be necessary. If she didn't agree, he wondered whether he would suggest that they just drop the session. He knew this might inhibit future sessions--and would not be greeted favorably by his supervisor!

QUESTIONS FOR DISCUSSION

1. What do you think of Robert's solution? How would you expect Judy to respond? If you were Robert's supervisor, what would be your reaction if Robert and Judy decided to terminate library instruction for her course?

2. Student evaluations of instructors are usually anonymous, in order to encourage more honest responses. Robert's faculty evaluations are not anonymous. Discuss the validity and usefulness of asking classroom teachers to evaluate librarians in this manner.

3. Robert and Judy appear to disagree about the amount of control the librarian has over the content of an instructional session. How would you respond to Robert's dismay over the professor's views? To what degree should a librarian follow his or her own ideas versus those of the faculty member?

4. Robert receives evaluations from students, faculty, and himself. How would you assess the relative weights he or his supervisor should assign to these different sources?

5. Assume that Robert has faculty status at his institution. How appropriate is it for him to submit to evaluations by other faculty for his instructional sessions? Do you think this type of evaluation will increase or decrease the "status" of librarians among the other faculty?

6. What other methods of evaluation by faculty might be useful for an instructional librarian? Consider their effects in terms of improving both library instruction and the faculty/librarian political relationship.

ADDITIONAL READING

Baker, Betsy. "Bibliographic Instruction: Building the Librarian/Faculty Partnership." In *Integrating Library Use Skills into the General Curriculum*, edited by Maureen Pastine and Bill Katz, p. 311-28. New York: Haworth, 1989. (Also published as *The Reference Librarian*, no. 24, 1989).

Farber, Evan. "Librarian-Faculty Communication Techniques." In *Proceedings from Southeastern Conference on Approaches to Bibliographic Instruction, March 16-17, 1978*, edited by Cerise Oberman-Soroka, p. 71-79. Charleston, South Carolina: Continuing Education Office, College of Charleston, 1978.

Gore, Daniel. "Something There is That Doesn't Love: A Professor." *Library Journal* 104 (April 1982): 686-91.

McCarthy, Constance. "The Faculty Problem." *Journal of Academic Librarianship* 11 (July 1985): 142-45.

SELF-EVALUATION OF INSTRUCTION LIBRARIANS

SELF-EVALUATION: A SCHOOL LIBRARIAN'S DILEMMA

Mary Nofsinger

With shaking hands, Amanda Lee carefully wiped the sweat from her ashen face as her mind raced over the events of the past hour. She had just returned to her office in the Aurora High School Media Center after a conference with the principal, Mrs. Wetzel, regarding her performance evaluation for the past year. Since this was her first year as a school library media specialist, she had not really known what to expect. Mrs. Wetzel's final shocking words echoed in her ears: "Unless your performance improves significantly next year, your contract will *not* be renewed."

In somewhat of a daze, Amanda managed to make it through another busy Friday afternoon, working with students, teachers, and Media Center staff. The next day, she sat down to analyze seriously the principal's comments regarding her performance. Pulling Mrs. Wetzel's written review from her briefcase, Amanda read it carefully, point by point, including the statement at the bottom that the person being evaluated was responsible for presenting documentation of professional achievements. She also noted an area for her comments and signature, indicating that the review had been completed.

Gritting her teeth, Amanda angrily muttered, "I'm not going to accept this unsatisfactory review. It doesn't accurately reflect the work I have been doing with teachers or my relationships with students, parents, and staff." She shook her head. "The principal doesn't really seem to know what I do as a school librarian." Carefully studying the main categories of her performance evaluation form, Amanda noticed that it primarily dealt with teaching skills and objectives, the curriculum, and relationships with students, staff, and parents. "I'll be darned," she thought aloud, "this looks like an evaluation form just for *teachers*. It doesn't even mention the Media Center or my specific duties and responsibilities. Hmmm . . . . ." Quickly, she picked up a pencil and began to jot down a list of tasks she had accomplished this last year which related to the performance criteria listed on the form, as well as a supplementary list of duties unique to school library media specialists.

Amanda reflected on the first category, *Teaching Skills and Objectives*. "Sure wish I had learned more about teaching in library school. Somehow I just didn't realize how important it would be until now." She suddenly remembered that the principal had casually dropped by the Media Center several times early in the year when she had still been in the process of learning effective teaching techniques. "Gosh, now I know why Mrs. Wetzel rated me so poorly! I probably should have invited her to observe my class presentations this Spring. They have become much better. In fact, several teachers have made favorable comments about my teaching effectiveness."

Turning her mind to teaching objectives, Amanda realized that she had only a mental list of objectives related to her major duties and responsibilities. "Maybe I should develop specific, *written* performance objectives for myself," she pondered. "Then Mrs. Wetzel would have a better basis for evaluating my accomplishments each year. These could also clearly demonstrate how I contribute to school and district goals."

Feeling less apprehensive, Amanda continued on to the next category, *Support for the Curriculum*. "Gosh," she thought, "I've already done a tremendous amount in this area. Why, I have worked extensively with different teachers, providing library instruction to social studies, English, and history classes." She also remembered that she had taught several sections on term papers and had developed bibliographies of library materials for art, physical education, and geography classes. Last week, she had just finished compiling reading lists of historical fiction by school grade levels. Furthermore, she realized that the materials purchased for the Media Center reflected the curriculum needs of teachers. "I even notify faculty and students of new materials available here and in the District Media Center," she stated indignantly.

Amanda proceeded to the other categories on the evaluation form and made notes on her contributions. During this process, she realized that many of the duties she performed were not included on the evaluation form. "There isn't any specific place to note my statistics on the quantity of materials purchased, classified, cataloged, and circulated." She mentally noted that the annual inventory of materials and equipment had just been successfully completed on time. "It's amazing! These things weren't even mentioned in my performance evaluation yesterday. Furthermore, I'm going to ask my principal to contact the District Media Supervisor for his evaluation of my performance." With increasing confidence, she mused, "What else should I discuss with Mrs. Wetzel on Monday morning?"

QUESTIONS FOR DISCUSSION

1. How can a school library media specialist ensure that the principal is fully aware of a librarian's duties and responsibilities, and how these relate to school and district goals?

2. Discuss specific objectives for school library media specialists. Brainstorm on some approaches to modifying school district evaluation forms so that the contributions of school librarians are acknowledged.

3. How might a school library media specialist demonstrate his or her teaching skills to the principal, both formally and informally?

4. Discuss effective techniques for soliciting faculty, staff, student, and parental evaluation of school library media specialists.

5. What are some ways that a school's only media specialist could seek out support and evaluation from others?

ADDITIONAL READING

American Association of School Librarians. *Guidelines for Performance Appraisal of School Library Media Specialists.* Chicago: American Library Association, 1988.

American Association of School Librarians. *Information Power: Guidelines for School Library Media Programs.* Chicago: American Library Association; Association for Educational Communications & Technology, 1988.

American Association of School Librarians. *NCATE Guidelines for School Library Media Specialists: Basic Preparation.* Chicago: American Library Association, 1988.

Barron, Daniel D. "Communicating What SLM Specialists Do: The Evaluation Process." *School Library Journal* 33 (March 1987): 95-99.

Pfister, Fred C., and Nelson Towle. "A Practical Model for a Developmental Appraisal Program for School Library Media Specialists." *School Library Media Quarterly* 11 (Winter 1983): 111-21.

Pfister, Fred C., Joyce P. Vincelette, and Jonnie Sprimont. "An Integrated Performance Evaluation and Program Evaluation System." *School Library Media Quarterly* 14 (Winter 1986): 61-66.

Turner, Philip. *Helping Teachers Teach: A School Library Media Specialist's Role.* Littleton, Colorado: Libraries Unlimited, 1985.

Yesner, Bernice L., and Hilda L. Jay. *The School Administrator's Guide to Evaluating Library Media Programs.* Hamden, Conn.: Library Professional Publications, 1987.

CAN YOU TEACH AN OLD DOG NEW TRICKS? BI IN A SPECIAL LIBRARY

Carolyn Tynan

Lisa Stewart was excited about her new position with Smith Jones, a Big Eight accounting firm. She had been hired to manage the library of a regional office of this firm. The firm's office was located in the downtown section of a large city. The firm had three divisions and employed 500 people. The majority of the employees were professional accountants and consultants. There was a pool of secretaries and receptionists and also a small group of other professionals including the librarian, the personnel managers and office managers of each division, the marketing staff, and the computer support staff.

On Lisa's first day, Jeff Gregg, the Personnel Manager, discussed the library with her and the expectations of the Tax Division Managing Partner, George Williams. "George is particular about the library and likes it just so," Jeff told Lisa. "He believes the library is important to the Tax Division and he is the person responsible for the library budget. The library is located within the Tax Department, but it also serves the Audit and Consulting Divisions."

The Smith Jones Library was a one-person operation that consisted mainly of loose-leaf tax services. There was a dedicated LEXIS workstation and a collection of annual reports in disorganized piles. No reference collection or access to other online databases existed. Jeff had assured Lisa that the firm would support the library and improved access to materials.

Lisa also learned that the library was previously staffed by an incompetent nonprofessional. As a result, the firm had only minimal expectations for library services.

Lisa met with George to discuss the library and its budget. When she asked to make several purchases and justified them to George's satisfaction, they were approved. Lisa could see that she faced a second problem, the lack of a budget for the library over which she had responsibility. She had to go to George for approval of all expenditures. Lisa could see that getting approval for tax materials would not be a problem, but that it was going to be difficult for other materials. She soon learned there was also a problem of perception. Due to the Tax Partner's responsibility for the library expenditures and the library's location on the Tax Division floor, the Audit and Consulting Divisions felt that the library was strictly a tax library. Therefore, they did not look to the library for help locating information.

As Lisa became more familiar with the firm and the library, it became apparent that the Tax Division needed assistance locating recently published information and help searching LEXIS. Most of the tax staff using the library were one or two years out of school and were assigned the research work. Often, they didn't have any idea where to look for the information they were assigned to locate. Lisa worked one-on-one with them. They were pleased to receive the help and were satisfied with the service. However, each summer brought a group of new hires who were not familiar with the library or with tax research. Those who had been doing the research now moved on to other assignments and the new hires became the researchers. This was true of all three divisions in the firm.

Lisa set up an appointment with the Managing Partner of the Consulting Division. She discussed the library and asked for any suggestions from him regarding services they would need. He had none and told her that they felt that the "library was a tax library and really had no services of use to the Consulting Division." Lisa tried to explain the potential of the library, but was left feeling that everything she had said had fallen on deaf ears.

By working one-on-one with the staff in the tax department and by attempting to reach out to the Consulting Division, Lisa felt she was making some progress, though it was only with those that already used the library. But she was frustrated by the lack of knowledge of the sources demonstrated by even the tax staff and decided to do something about it.

28

Since the Tax Division was committed to the library, she decided to focus on instructing its staff in basic research skills. As she had noticed, the new hires and tax staff lacked skills in locating current information on changes in tax law. Lisa developed an hour-long presentation focusing on the sources for current information and how to use them. She then approached George with her idea for the instruction session. It was agreed that Lisa could give the session in one of the firm's classrooms and tax staff could voluntarily sign up for the session. George indicated that he wanted feedback from Lisa about the presentation. Out of fifty on staff, ten attended. Lisa was hoping more would attend, but it was a start.

Searching LEXIS was also a problem for most of the tax staff. It was used frequently by the staff and most wanted to search the database themselves. Without training, the staff were not searching the system effectively and efficiently. Rather than offer a formal session, Lisa posted times that she would be available to work with a staff member or small group specifically on LEXIS searching techniques and the different databases available. She felt that the staff might be more likely to take advantage of the service if they could come when they had a need to search the system and could get hands-on experience.

The presentation on current tax sources and the LEXIS sessions for the tax staff gave Lisa additional contact with that division, but she still did not have many users from the Audit and Consulting Divisions. In order to reach those divisions, she needed some publicity about the library and its services. Through her contacts in the marketing department, Lisa secured some space in the internal newsletter to promote the library.

Lisa believed that she was making some progress, but she needed to evaluate the success of what she had done up to this point before she proceeded with any additional programs. George required feedback about the instruction session, but she was unsure about where and how to start the process of evaluation.

QUESTIONS FOR DISCUSSION

1. Who should Lisa ask to evaluate the success of her programs? Should it be a formal evaluation by the entire firm, just the tax division, or just those that have participated in the programs?

2. What should she evaluate? What questions should she ask? What methods should she use?

3. Given the disinterest of the Audit and Consulting Divisions, how could the evaluation method be structured to encourage comments about needed services and resources? How could it be structured to inform as well as evaluate?

4. How could Lisa measure the success of her efforts to publicize the library through the Smith Jones newsletter? What would be the advantages and disadvantages of a separate library newsletter?

5. Those staff with authority in the firm do not perceive any direct benefits from using the library or from library instruction. How can Lisa develop additional support for her instruction efforts?

6. Should any kind of library instruction be required? Who should be required to participate? How should Lisa approach the partners about requiring library instruction?

ADDITIONAL READING

Hubbard, Abigail, and Barbara Wilson. "An Integrated Information Management
    Program... Defining a New Role for Librarians in Helping End-Users." *Online*
    10 (March 1986): 15-23.

Thury, Eva M. "From Library to Information Center: Case Studies in the Evolution of
    Corporate Information Resources." *Special Libraries* 79 (Winter 1988): 21-27.

Wagenveld, Linda M. "Doing More With Less." *Special Libraries* 78 (Winter 1987): 16-20.

Zachert, Martha Jane. "The Information Manager as Provider of Educational Services."
    Special Libraries 80 (Summer 1989): 193-97.

Zachert, Martha Jane, and Robert V. Williams. "Marketing Measures for Information
    Services." *Special Libraries* 77 (Spring 1986): 61-70.

SPECIAL EVALUATION SITUATIONS

EVALUATING SIGN SYSTEMS

Trish Ridgeway

As she surveyed the piles of paper on her desk, Juanita sighed and reached for her Diet Coke. *A two-week vacation isn't worth it!* she thought to herself. *Not when this mess is waiting. Well, at least I'm halfway through sorting, and the trash pile is the tallest stack! Oh, no, a memo from the big boss. I hope this isn't too bad . . .* She began reading the memo:

To: Juanita Lopez,
         Bibliographic Instruction Coordinator

From: Alberta Lentz,
         Director of Library Services

Re: Library Signage

Since your job description includes coordination of all library instruction and orientation activities at Upper West State College, I am giving you the additional responsibility of library signage. Our current system was set up ten years ago and has been sadly neglected. Under your capable leadership I'm sure we can institute an effective system that can be constantly reviewed, evaluated, and changed as needed.

I have appointed a committee (see the names listed below) to work with you initially because your first task is big--to evaluate how our current signage looks and works, in order to decide whether to modify it or start over from scratch. Of course, our funds for this project are not unlimited, but don't let monetary considerations hinder you unduly. There is money available for signage from the college Planning and Design Office. After my

32

review of your recommendations, the committee will then bring its plans to fruition.

One of the reasons our current system of signage has not been satisfactory is that Jim Fenzi, who designed it, left shortly after it was installed, and no one else took responsibility. As you know, we have a visual mess--hand-lettered signs everywhere, corrections pasted over our original signs, missing letters on signs, missing signs, and no clear indication of whether the signs and floorplans are fulfilling the purposes for which they were designed.

You know how strongly I feel about evaluating the effectiveness of our programs; from the outset be certain your committee designs a system that can be periodically reviewed and changed to meet current needs.

Please have an evaluation of the current system and your committee's initial recommendations ready for me in six months. Feel free to come in and discuss with me your committee's questions, concerns, etc., whenever you wish.

"Signage!" Juanita hissed. "I hate that word, and what does it have to do with bibliographic instruction? Ugh!"

She sat fuming, listing to herself all the reasons she shouldn't be in charge of library signage: *Number one, I have no artistic ability. Two, I hate signage. Three, no one ever reads signs anyway. Four, I hate signage. Five, how can you evaluate how well signage works? Follow people around the building? Six, I hate signage. Seven, I'm too busy!*

Later in the day, Juanita met Frank Harries, the Head of Reference at Upper West, for lunch. "Frank, you're on this signage committee, too. I wish Alberta didn't think signage has some connection to BI!"

Frank looked surprised. "You don't? Our main aim in orientation is to help people find their way around. Isn't that what a sign system does?"

"Okay, I know you're right, but why me? I have no interest or talent in this area, and the job is enormous. I have no idea where to start. It's been ten years since the addition to the main building was finished, and no one has been able to find a way to help people get from the old part to the new section. I don't think any sign system can help people understand that you can get to level 2 of the addition from level 2 of the stacks but that you can't get from level 1 of the addition to level 1 of the stacks! And the difficulty of creating a system that can be constantly evaluated. . . . I feel so overwhelmed by this task!"

Frank grimaced. "I agree it's a big job; but since we have to do it anyway, I'd prefer to look at it as a challenge. Where do you think we should start?"

QUESTIONS FOR DISCUSSION

1. Should signage be the responsibility of the person who handles bibliographic instruction?

2. Where would you begin to work on this project?

3. How would you evaluate the current system of signage?

4. How would you set up a signage program that could be regularly evaluated and updated?

5. Are librarians the appropriate people to create signs, or is it justifiable to hire graphic artists, environmental designers, or other specialists?

ADDITIONAL READING

Kupersmith, John. "'Library Anxiety' and Library Graphics." *Research Strategies* 5 (Winter 1987): 36-41.

_____. "Why Bother with a Sign System?" *Research Strategies* 1 (Winter 1983): 33-35.

Mallery, Mary S., and Ralph E. DeVore. *A Sign System for Libraries.* Chicago: American Library Association, 1982.

Pollet, Dorothy, and Peter Haskell. *Sign Systems for Libraries: Solving the Way Finding Problem.* New York: Bowker, 1979. (See especially the chapter, "Evaluating Signage Systems in Libraries," by John Lubans, Jr. and Gary Kushner, p. 115-23.)

Reynold, Linda, and Stephen Barett. *Signs and Guiding for Libraries.* London: Bingley, 1981.

SCISSORS, PAPER, STONE:
EVALUATING PRINTED MATERIALS USED IN A PUBLIC LIBRARY

Mary Pagliero Popp

Tom Hilton sat at his desk, staring off into space. His head was pounding. He had just left a meeting of department and branch heads in the Raccoon County Public Library system. There he had been given a new task that everyone was sure was "just right" for the new Head of the Reference Department in the Main Library. What that really meant was no one else wanted to do it. Since he had been at Raccoon County only eight months, Tom had known he was going to get stuck with the job.

Today was June 19. By July 15, Tom had to bring back to the group a plan to evaluate and revise the printed handouts Raccoon County was using to help patrons work with the new online catalog.

Raccoon County Public Library

Raccoon County Public Library is located in a semi-rural area in southern Illinois. It serves the county seat, Jasonville, a city of 45,000, as well as two smaller towns. Each of the two smaller towns has a branch library.

Most of the people in Raccoon County are skilled workers. There are two large manufacturing plants in the area. A number of residents are farmers. A small church-affiliated college enrolling about 650 students is located in Jasonville. The population in the county is getting older; more than 30% of the residents are over 65. Yet many young people have stayed in the area to raise families. Enrollment in the three elementary schools in the area has been booming.

The Automation Project

The library system has purchased a computerized catalog and circulation system from a major commercial vendor. About 70% of the library's collection has been converted and put into the online catalog, including children's materials and nonprint items, but much of the adult nonfiction collection is still not in the online catalog.

The main library has seven computer terminals for patron use. Two of these are in the children's collection. One of the branch libraries has two terminals; the other has only one.

Printed Materials

Tom went out to the reference area and took inventory of what the library had already done. There were signs on each terminal telling users that the catalog existed, that it was not complete, and that they should use the card catalog for older materials. The signs described how to look up authors, titles and subjects. They stood up on tables next to the terminals and were colorful. All of the print was done in red ink.

A three-fold printed handout was available in the handout rack. It contained brief descriptions of searching by author, title and subject, and sample screens. The print was small, especially on the sample screens.

Tom looked across the library. The Children's Department had made a display about the new computer catalog. It had originally been colorful, but it had been up for seven months now and was starting to fade.

Tom wondered what the branch libraries had done to tell users about the catalog.

Getting Help

The more Tom thought, the more he realized that he could not handle this project alone. He was going to need lots of help, particularly from the branch librarians and the children's librarians.

Tom also realized that he did not know whether patrons actually used the signs or the printed brochure. If they did use them, did patrons get the answers they needed?

Money

In order to acquire attractive materials, Tom knew that he would need to spend money--get good paper, use attractive colors, perhaps hire a graphic designer. What sort of budget would be available? Tom wrote this down as another question to ask.

A First Step

Tom picked up the phone and made a call to the director's office. He made an appointment for the day after tomorrow. Now he really had to think. What should he say to the director? What questions should he ask?

QUESTIONS FOR DISCUSSION

1. List the key points that Tom should discuss in his initial meeting with the director.

2. How can Tom get other librarians in the system involved in the planning effort? What would be the advantages and disadvantages of wider involvement?

3. How should instructional materials for children differ from those aimed at teenagers? How should materials for children and teenagers differ from those designed for adults?

4. How could Tom get some input from users? What users should he ask for help? How can Tom test whether the printed materials answer the questions of users?

5. What should printed materials accomplish in order to introduce users to an online catalog?

6. What criteria should be used to evaluate printed materials?

7. What is a reasonable timetable for an effort of this sort?

ADDITIONAL READING

Burbank, Lucille, and Dennis Pett. "Designing Printed Instructional Materials."
Performance and Instruction Journal 25 (October 1986): 5-9.

Frick, Elizabeth. "Theories of Learning and Their Impact on OPAC Instruction."
Research Strategies 7 (Spring 1989): 67-78.

Hooten, Patricia. "Online Catalogs: Will They Improve Children's Access?" *Journal of
Youth Services in Libraries* 2 (Spring 1989): 267-72.

Kupersmith, John. "A Design Model for Instructional Graphics." *Research Strategies* 2
(Summer 1984): 136-38.

____. "Tradeoffs in Designing Library Graphics." *Research Strategies* 6 (Winter 1988):
33-35.

Lawson, Patricia. "Effective Instructional Materials Are More Than Content."
Performance and Instruction Journal 25 (1986): 3-4.

Liebold, Louise Condak. *Fireworks, Brass Bands, and Elephants: Promotional Events with
a Flair for Libraries and Other Nonprofit Organizations*. Phoenix: Oryx Press, 1986.
(See especially chapter 7, "Publicity and the Media.")

BURNOUT AND BI

Sally Lyon

Margaret, Head of the Reference Division at Mid-City College Library, had experienced a staff reduction of one-third last semester when two reference librarians retired and another went on a one-year research leave. Due to a college-wide hiring freeze, it would be some time before replacements would be hired for the two positions left open by retirements.

Bibliographic instruction is taught by the librarians in the Reference Division. Because of the reduction in staff, each librarian has had to take on more BI classes, as well as additional hours at the Reference Desk.

As the Fall Semester was coming to a close, Margaret was aware of the toll this increased workload had taken on her staff. She and her once eager staff were beginning to show less interest in their BI presentations. The enthusiasm and spark they once had was gone. Additionally, staff absences were increasing. All the signs of burnout were present.

The Library was planning to convert soon to an online catalog, which would bring some need for additional instruction. Margaret was presently trying to get funds and technical assistance to produce a video on the Library and the new online catalog to use for individual and class orientations. If and when the video was produced, it would relieve her staff from repetitious instruction and allow them to use their time and energy to instruct students in more specific aspects of library use and research. But the video would not be produced in time to relieve the Division's present problem.

Margaret remembered a conversation she had with the new Head of Technical Services, Bob, soon after he joined the library staff. He had expressed interest in teaching basic library instruction classes. Maybe other librarians in Technical Services would also like to participate in BI. They could supply needed relief to the beleaguered reference staff; it would also be a good time to get the Reference and Technical Services librarians together to plan for instruction for the new online catalog. She decided to discuss her ideas with her staff at their next division meeting.

At the meeting, Margaret presented her idea of making an instructional video of the Library and discussed the offer from the Head of Technical Services to teach BI classes. Strong opinions quickly poured out from the librarians.

"I like the idea of making a video on the Library, especially since we can include the online catalog, and it will save us from having to repeat the same information again and again. Also, our students will love learning about the Library from a video."

"Making an instructional video sounds great and getting help from our colleagues in Technical Services sounds even better. Let them see how much time and effort it takes to plan and teach students who are not always attentive!"

"Great," spoke out a third librarian. "Where do we find the time to make a video? We have too much to do now! I say we should cut down on the number of BI classes we teach--or better yet not hold any until we get back to full staffing."

"The librarians in Technical Services have too much work already to give us help with BI. Anyway, they are inexperienced in teaching and don't know the library's resources as well as we do," said another reference librarian. "Perhaps we should cut down on the hours of reference service in order to continue to offer BI. Remember, the more students we instruct in a group, the less individual instruction we need to give later at the Reference Desk."

As Margaret listened to the comments of her staff, she realized that perhaps her ideas for handling the division's BI problems might not be the best or only solutions. Although all of her staff did not agree with her proposals, they had at least opened up and spoken out. They had had the opportunity to express their frustrations and share their ideas. Margaret felt that even though they did not reach a solution to their present problem, this meeting had brought about an exchange of ideas and a good starting point to tackle their problems.

QUESTIONS FOR DISCUSSION

1. Given the emotional state of most of her staff, should Margaret have presented her ideas for BI as she did or should she have just gone ahead and implemented them?

2. Is asking colleagues in Technical Services to help with BI just a quick stop-gap measure or is it an opportunity for Reference and Technical Services librarians to work together? What might be the positive and negative consequences of such collaboration?

3. Will the production of an instructional video bring some relief or just create another skill the staff needs to learn?

4. Should the staff decrease the number of BI classes taught, or perhaps not even offer them until additional librarians can be hired? Should the Reference Desk hours be cut instead?

5. Will it do more harm than good to have tired, uninspired librarians teaching BI?

6. How might the BI problem at Mid-City College Library be addressed while simultaneously addressing the problem of staff burnout? Without addressing the burnout issue, can anything be done to solve the Library's problems?

7. What other ways could this problem be handled?

ADDITIONAL READING

Elliott, J. L., and N. M. Smith. "Burnout: A Look at Coping with Stress." *School Library Media Quarterly* 12 (Winter 1984): 136, 141-45.

Fimian, Michael J., Sandra A. Benedit and Stacie Johnson. "The Measure of Occupational Stress and Burnout Among Library Media Specialists." *Library and Information Science Research* 11 (January 1989): 3-19.

Intner, Sheila. "BI and the Technical Service Librarian." *Technicalities* 6 (January 1986): 7-10.

Nauratil, M. J. "Causes and Cures: Librarian Burnout and Alienation." *Canadian Library Journal* 44 (December 1987): 385-89.

Roose, Tina, Mary Haack and John W. Jones. "Occupational Burnout Among Librarians." *Drexel Library Quarterly* 20 (Spring 1984): 46-72.

Roose, Tina. "Stress at the Reference Desk." *Library Journal* 114 (September 1989): 166-67.

SERVICE WITH A SMILE: STRESS AND EVALUATION IN A PUBLIC LIBRARY

Valerie Feinman

"Service!" she said, as she held her head and tried not to laugh out loud. Choked laughter was the only way she could deal with this most recent criticism. "I wonder what he thinks we are doing out here while he hides in his paneled cage. I have two librarians on the reference desk, another at the information desk, and I'm trouble-shooting in the area. There are never more than two people lined up for each librarian; we are actually helping people at a fairly good rate. Now he wants smiles too?" Meet Sue Brown, chief reference librarian for the Meadowlea Public Library system. The Director, Michael Redfern, has been at Meadowlea for almost one year.

Meadowlea is a bustling community of 46,000, located 20 miles from a major city. The public library has several branches as well as the main building, Mainlea. Most serious reference work is done at Mainlea. The community supports its libraries well, but also makes demands. Hours in Mainlea reflect a population which heavily uses its amenities during evenings and weekends. The schools are highly rated nationally and send 85% of their graduates to college. Students perform fairly sophisticated research in their search for entrance to top schools. Thus the library bustles after school lets out and on weekends.

Sunday afternoons are the most popular library hours. Lonely older residents come out for fresh air and the chance of meeting friends. They are avid readers, watching the best seller list very carefully. Busy adults take a brief time out to check out the collection of magazines or find a book for reading on the train. Young children accompany older siblings or adults or grandparents, are easily bored, and run around the several rooms. Teenagers pretend to study while watching each other, and generally hang out. During much of the school year, young adults take over the reference room with their projects.

The librarians often feel that the number of students performing each task is infinite.

Library instruction is offered on demand and by appointment, as well as one afternoon and one evening weekly, as announced in the library newsletter received by all residents. The weekly sessions have a standard format, but are easily geared to interests of any particular group, whether this consists of seniors, book clubbers or students. School classes are encouraged to visit, but the high school librarians think that they have trained their students well enough not to need additional help. In most cases this is true, and the ability of students to help themselves is not a problem.

Some communities prefer high school students to use their school library for most assignments, but often the school is not open when demand is highest. Meadowlea students may have jobs or may be active in sports or take music lessons. Clubs and choirs and teams meet daily after classes finish. Therefore Mainlea receives most of the homework problems.

Each fall when school begins, Sue sends a letter to each teacher in the high school, describing the services offered and requesting a "homework alert" for particularly heavy assignments. She encourages them to send her reading lists and assignment sheets, and asks that the teachers actually check library holdings before sending whole classes in. She also requests that teachers ask their students to provide photocopies, rather than original illustrations, to accompany papers; this is a reminder that students sometimes prefer to cut out pictures when requested to provide them. She has regular talks with the school librarians, who also provide information on assignments. Generally the system works fairly well.

Individual projects can cause problems. One student insisted he needed a picture of a chicken skeleton, because he had deboned one and was reconstructing the bird. Eventually the needed picture was found. Another student needed Livy in both Latin and English--not everyday reading in most small libraries.

If a teacher calls ahead to warn the librarians that 25 students are coming in to use Vergil, and the library buys extra copies and hands them out for limited use, and study groups are set up to handle the volume, then of course another school will give the same assignment without notifying the library at all. The parent of the first student who cannot find a copy of Vergil immediately calls up Sue's boss and fills his ear with unwarranted criticism.

"Forecasting was not one of the talents I was asked about when they hired me, and I am being evaluated on its lack," moaned Sue.

Each fall, history classes come in to use pre-War maps of Europe. Each fall, Sue removes the historical atlases containing the needed maps from the reference shelves and places them behind the desk where they must be signed out. Each fall, one or more atlases are mutilated or stolen. Sue has called the teacher who assigns this map study to enlist his help in speaking to his students about theft and mutilation. He insists that his students can find all the needed information in their textbooks. Of course they can, but they would rather use the pictorial representation. Some years she has handed out copies of the needed map, but feels this is not an ideal solution.

Some assignments completely stump the librarians. One social studies teacher requested several pages of background data on each of twenty Dutch explorers. Librarians found minimal paragraphs on five. In this case the teacher had assumed the library could cope and was most surprised when his frustrated students were unable to complete their papers. He obviously felt the library in this community would have all that anyone needed and deemed it quite unnecessary to communicate. When this happens, everyone is unhappy. Librarians are frustrated because they can't help. Redfern is furious that his staff can't foresee all needs and take action. Parents are unhappy because they pay taxes so the library will have "everything." Teachers are unhappy because they look foolish in their choice of assignments. The library board is unhappy because residents complain. Redfern is again unhappy because the board complains to him. This is a no-win situation, and Sue Brown is the chief recipient of all agonies.

Evaluation of the library program is performed on many levels; some of these are more important than others. One unhappy parent or student should not mark the downfall of a librarian. There is, however, an ongoing evaluation by the community which is not considered officially in the review of Sue's professional responsibilities.

Beyond the problems occurring with difficult assignments, there is an enormous behavior problem. Many students use the library daily as an extension of their family room. They congregate after school to work on homework and are still there several hours later. This is too long a period of quiet activity, and yet when parents arrive to provide rides home, students are unwilling to leave. They are, of course, not working much of the time. The situation can be rather noisy and rude, and many adult library patrons simply leave or do not use the library on those evenings. Sue is never certain whether she should be delighted that the students are using the collection or disappointed that she is not a social worker or policewoman. The Director is happy to see heavy use, but he doesn't understand noisy teenagers. Adult users are beginning to complain.

Redfern has simple rules for his staff: lines must be short and attractive smiles must be visible. He is more authoritarian than helpful, and generally does not provide constructive criticism to his employees. His evaluation of programs is based more upon community use and the few opinions reported to him than on any study of work actually being done by his staff. Yet he continues to demand service with a smile.

QUESTIONS FOR DISCUSSION

1. Should public librarians evaluate school assignments? Why or why not? If so, how might this be done? When the needs of the library conflict with those of the schools, how may this be resolved?

2. How might the library evaluate its outreach to schools? What follow-up should be done?

3. When a parent complained bitterly to Redfern about her child's inability to find specific information, he passed on the complaint to Sue and stated: "It should not happen again. The materials budget is more than adequate. The Board should not hear complaints." Sue found this treatment unreasonable and requested discussion from her side. How could she create a more equitable process of evaluation by her supervisor?

4. Would more library instruction be useful in solving or preventing behavior problems? What if it contained a small segment on how to behave in a library? How would you set this up?

5. Should one parental complaint outweigh otherwise excellent service? What about three complaints? How might Sue ensure that representative feedback on the quality of service be gathered?

ADDITIONAL READING

Eaton, E. Gale. "What the Public Children's Librarian Needs to Know About Locational Skills Instruction in Elementary Schools." *Journal of Youth Services in Libraries* 2 (Summer 1989): 357-66.

Fitzgibbons, Shirley. "Cooperation Between Teachers, School Librarians, and Public Librarians: Improving Library Services for Children and Young Adults." *Indiana Libraries* 8 (no. 1, 1989): 57-69.

Haycock, Ken. "Beyond Courtesy: School and Public Library Relationships." *Emergency Librarian* 16 (May/June 1989): 27-30. (Includes excellent checklist.)

Jones, Patrick, and Candace E. Morse. "What To Do When the *World Book* Is Missing: A Program of Public Library Instruction for High School Students." *RQ* 26 (Fall 1986): 31-34.

Monroe, J. W. "The Hanged One, or, Turning Things Topsy-Turvy." *Voice of Youth Advocates* 11 (April 1988): 17-19.

Toifel, Ronald C., and Wesley D. Davis. "Investigating Library Study Skills of Children in the Public Schools." *Journal of Academic Librarianship* 9 (September 1983): 211-15.

Wood, Judy B., J. J. Bremer, and S. A. Saraidarides. "Measurement of Service at a Public Library." *Public Library Quarterly* 2 (Summer 1980): 49-57.

THE APPLICATION OF EVALUATION

PAYING LIP SERVICE TO EVALUATION: DO YOU FOLLOW THROUGH?

Scott Davis

John sat at his computer, opened the last envelope of the day's mail, and removed the completed questionnaire that had been returned to him by a school librarian. John had worked as a secondary school library media specialist for three years when he decided to return to graduate school for a doctorate in education. The dissertation process was now in full swing.

Having been actively involved in library instruction while working as a school media specialist, John had chosen library instruction as his doctoral research area. His study focused on the scope of secondary school library instruction in five southern states. One of the primary research questions in his study concerned evaluation of library instruction efforts. He had included several items on his research questionnaire that would solicit data about how school librarians evaluate their library instruction activities, e.g. written student evaluations, written teacher evaluations, self-evaluation, student scores, etc. There were also items on the questionnaire that asked school librarians how they use evaluation results to improve their instruction programs.

In the course of entering questionnaire data over the last several days, John had become very conscious of the school librarians' responses to the items which dealt with the frequency of evaluation and how evaluation results were used. Most respondents reported that they conduct some form of library instruction evaluation; however, a noticeable number of school librarians were indicating that they did not evaluate their library instruction program in any structured way. John was anxious to see what the statistical analysis would finally tell about program evaluation.

Within six weeks John had finished compiling the data. In regard to secondary school library instruction evaluation, John's data yielded the following:

1. Two hundred three school librarians (79%) indicated that their library instruction program was evaluated in some way. Fifty-five school librarians (21%) reported that there was no evaluation procedure for their program.

2. The most common form of evaluation used by school librarians was student scores/performance on library skills exercises and tests (66%). The second most common form of evaluation for library instruction was self-evaluation (51%).

3. Thirty-four percent of the school librarians indicated that their library instruction efforts were evaluated only once a year. Another 34% reported that they included some form of evaluation after every library instruction activity. Seven percent never evaluated their program. Others indicated varying frequencies, from once a month to three times per year.

4. Seventy-two percent of the school librarians indicated that their library instruction program had been revised as a result of evaluation data; 14% reported that their library instruction program had never been revised based on evaluation results.

Even though John was trying to remain unbiased in reacting to his findings, he was dumbfounded that there were any school librarians who were **not** evaluating their instruction program in some way (see item #1). And what about the 14% who did conduct evaluations, but had never modified their program based on evaluation results? Were their programs perfect, or were their evaluation instruments invalid?

QUESTIONS FOR DISCUSSION

1. Assuming that John's study is reliable, do John's findings mesh with your own experiences regarding program evaluation? Do you believe that many librarians just pay lip service to evaluation?

2. How could library science graduate programs address this problem? Based on your own training, do you feel that you received adequate training in the theory and mechanics of program evaluation?

3. Is it ever appropriate to exclude an evaluation component in an instructional activity?

4. In designing an evaluation instrument, one may subconsciously bias the evaluation so that one gets only those responses that one wants to hear, i.e., only the good things. How can this be avoided?

5. What types of evaluative input should school librarians solicit from students? from faculty members? from the school administration? Is one group's input necessarily more important than the others'?

6. Once an evaluation has been conducted, how should one follow through with the evaluation results? Who should the school librarian share evaluation results with and how?

7. While school librarians should show some initiative in the evaluation process, to what extent is program evaluation really the responsibility of the school administration?

8. Discuss the strengths and weaknesses of self-evaluation as a legitimate form of program evaluation.

ADDITIONAL READING

Baldwin, Margaret. "Evaluating High School Libraries: Service is Top Priority." *Catholic Library World* 54 (February 1988): 165-67.

Davis, H. Scott. *Library Instruction in Five Southern States*. Unpublished doctoral dissertation, East Texas State University, 1987.

Morey, T. Mark, and Jacqueline Reihman. "Data Management and Statistical Analysis." In *Evaluating Bibliographic Instruction: A Handbook*, p. 79-94. Chicago: American Library Association, 1983.

King, David N. "Evaluation and Its Uses." In *Evaluating Bibliographic Instruction: A Handbook*, p. 5-21. Chicago: American Library Association, 1983.

Waddle, Linda. "School Media Matters." *Wilson Library Bulletin* 62 (September 1987): 54-55.

Werking, Richard Hume. "The Place of Evaluation in Bibliographic Education." In *Proceedings from Southeastern Conference on Approaches to Bibliographic Instruction, March 16-17, 1978*, edited by Cerise Oberman-Soroka, p. 100-18. Charleston, South Carolina: Continuing Education Office, College of Charleston, 1978.

CONTRIBUTORS

Scott Davis, Ed. D., is Librarian/Head, Department of Library Instruction and Orientation, Indiana State University Libraries, Terre Haute, Indiana.

Valerie Feinman is Coordinator of Library Instruction, Adelphi University Libraries, Garden City, New York.

Rebecca Jackson is Coordinator for Instructional Services, University of Maryland at College Park, Maryland.

Sally Lyon is Chief of the Reference Division at the City College of New York, and also coordinates library instruction.

Mary Nofsinger is Head of Reference, Humanities/Social Sciences Library, Washington State University, Pullman, Washington.

Christopher W. Nolan is Reference Services Librarian, Trinity University, San Antonio, Texas.

Mary Pagliero Popp is Head, Library Instruction, Indiana University, Bloomington, Indiana.

Trish Ridgeway, a library consultant, is also an adjunct faculty member at Catholic University School of Library and Information Science and a doctoral student in higher education at George Washington University.

Carolyn Tynan is the Undergraduate Library Services Librarian for Collections and the Halls of Residence Libraries at Indiana University.

Other contributors: Additional editing assistance was provided by Suzanne Holler, Rebecca Jackson, Scott Davis, and Trish Ridgeway. Other committee members who gave input to this project include Ross Poli and Craig Gibson.

The Library Instruction Round Table (LIRT) of the American Library Association (ALA) provides a forum for discussing library instruction issues pertinent to all types of libraries. Among its other projects, the **LIRT Continuing Education Committee** has also published *Case Studies in Library Instruction*, revised edition (Chicago: Continuing Education Committee, LIRT, ALA, 1989). Requests for the purchase of copies may be sent to the LIRT staff liaison at the ALA office in Chicago (50 East Huron St., Chicago, IL 60611).

The LIRT Continuing Education Committee is most interested in your comments about this publication. If you found any sections especially stimulating, used these cases in an innovative way, or have suggestions for improving any later editions, please send your thoughts to:

LIRT Continuing Education Committee
c/o Jeniece Guy
American Library Association
50 E. Huron St.
Chicago, IL 60611